Paint by Numbers

by Marilyn Eden
illustrated by Darryl Ligason

 HOUGHTON MIFFLIN   BOSTON

Printed in China

ISBN 10: 0-618-90003-9
ISBN 13: 978-0-618-90003-9

789 0940 16 15 14 13

4500432010

Thomas and his Uncle Paul pulled up in front of the animal shelter. It was a beautiful day, but none of the animals were outside. They were all inside the shelter so they would not get in the way. Thomas and Uncle Paul had come to paint the front fence. They did not need wet noses and furry paws poking into the fresh paint!

Thomas loved animals. He wanted to spend the whole day playing with the animals that were waiting at the shelter to be adopted. Instead, he was going to spend the day painting the fence. Thomas hated painting, but he really liked Uncle Paul. When his uncle had asked for his help, Thomas couldn't say no.

After unloading the cans of paint and the brushes, Uncle Paul and Thomas inspected the fence. It was made of cement blocks. Each block was a square that measured 12 inches on each side.

"Hey," said Thomas, "that means that the perimeter of each cement square is 4 feet: 1 foot + 1 foot + 1 foot + 1 foot. It's 4 feet around the outside edges of the square."

"You're pretty smart," said Uncle Paul. "Now do you know how to figure out the area of that square? The square is 1 foot long and 1 foot wide. So, $1 \times 1 = 1$. Each time we paint one of these cement blocks, we will have painted 1 square foot."

"Cool," said Thomas. "Let's figure out how many square feet we're going to have to paint to cover the whole fence." He started counting each square block in the fence.

Read·Think·Write What is the perimeter of a figure?

"Hold on," Uncle Paul said. "I know a quicker way to find the area of this fence. Just count one row of blocks to see how long the fence is. Then count one column of blocks to see how tall the fence is."

The fence was 40 blocks long and 4 blocks tall. Because each block had 12-inch sides, that meant the fence was 40 feet long and 4 feet high.

Uncle Paul said, "Now just multiply the length times the height, and you'll find the area."

Read·Think·Write What is the area of the fence?

Thomas multiplied 40 feet × 4 feet in his head. "The area of this fence is 160 feet!" he announced.

"Almost right," Uncle Paul said. "The fence is 160 square feet. Area is always measured in squares. In this case, it happens to be square feet.

"If you're measuring the area of something very small, you might figure out how many centimeters long and high it is. Then you would say what the area was in square centimeters.

"If you were measuring the area of something very large, you might need to use miles. Then you would end up with square miles."

"I wish this fence were 160 square centimeters," frowned Thomas. "Then we'd already be done painting it."

Uncle Paul patted Thomas on the shoulder and said, "I appreciate your help, Thomas. You go ahead and start. I'll let the director know that we are here." Uncle Paul walked inside the shelter, leaving Thomas alone with the fence and a paintbrush.

Read·Think·Write How do you find the area of a figure?

Just then, Thomas's friend Chuck came walking by. Chuck was on his way to the pool. Thomas wished that he could go swimming, too.

"Hey, Chuck," Thomas called. "Would you help me paint this fence?"

Chuck stopped to see what Thomas was doing, which did not look like much fun. "I can't help you," he said. "I told my mom I was going to the pool, and I'll get in trouble if I don't show up there. Sorry!"

Chuck walked quickly toward the pool.

Thomas realized that he was going to have to think of another way to get someone to help him. He checked his pockets to see what he might be able to use to "pay" for some help. There wasn't much: a broken plastic whistle, a half-eaten apple (with a bit of lint stuck to it), and a penny.

Thomas painted two square feet of the fence. Then along came Rosita, riding her bike to the library. Thomas did things differently this time.

"Hi, Rosita!" he called.

"*Hola!*" Rosita said. "What are you doing?"

"I'm painting this fence," said Thomas. "Do you want to help? I'll pay you!"

"I don't know," Rosita replied. "How much?"

"I'll give you my lucky penny, and I'll let you have the rest of my apple." Thomas put the penny and the apple on the fence.

Rosita made a face when she saw the apple.

"Okay, this cool whistle, too," Thomas said.

Rosita looked at the whistle, the fence, and Thomas. "No, thanks," she said. "I really need to get these books back to the library."

Read·Think·Write Thomas has painted 2 square feet of the fence. How much more needs to be painted?

Uncle Paul was still inside the shelter, so it did not look as if Thomas was going to be getting any help from him. Thomas had only painted a couple more square feet of fence when he had an idea—a very good idea. Just then the Ramirez twins came by on their skateboards. They stopped to see what Thomas was doing.

Thomas pretended not to notice them at all. He acted as if he was very busy painting. He made a couple of careful brushstrokes on one of the squares, and then he stood back. He looked carefully at what he'd done.

"What are you doing?" asked Emilio.

"It looks hard," added Flora.

"I'm painting," Thomas said. "I'm practicing to become a famous fence artist. Now please don't bother me. This is very tricky." Thomas dabbed a little more paint on one of his squares.

"We want to try that!" the twins said together.

"Can we, please?" asked Flora.

"We'll be really careful," promised Emilio.

Thomas pretended to think about it. Finally, he said, "Well, I suppose it would okay. You can do some of the squares at the far end."

He gave Flora a paintbrush and some paint. Flora was going to paint a section of the fence that was 4 feet long and 4 feet high. Thomas directed Emilio to a section that was 8 feet long and 2 feet high.

The Ramirez twins were very excited. They each gave Thomas a super sour sucker to thank him for letting them become famous fence artists, too.

Read·Think·Write What area of the fence will both twins paint?

Before long, Thomas was not painting at all.
He was supervising. He had Kaya painting 10 square
feet of fence. He had Hamid painting 12 square feet.
Benjamin and Jenna were each painting 4 square feet.
In fact, kids were lined up, waiting for their turns
to paint.

Thomas was enjoying one of the super sour
suckers and looking over the new "payments" the
other kids had made to have a chance to paint. Along
with the suckers, Thomas now had a piece of chalk, a
red leaf, one black sock with a hole in it, and a rubber
band, among other things.

Thomas decided that he liked painting fences
after all.

Read·Think·Write How many square feet will Kaya,
Hamid, Benjamin, and Jenna paint?

Just as Thomas was cleaning up the paint and brushes, Uncle Paul came out of the shelter with the director.

"Wow!" he said. "I can't believe you're already done with this fence! I thought it would take us the whole afternoon."

"It's beautiful," the director said. "You have done a wonderful job, Thomas. The yard looks much better. Thank you for all your help."

"It wasn't hard at all," said Thomas. "When it comes to painting fences, you just have to know what you're doing. It's all in the numbers."

1. Summarize How can you find the perimeter of a figure?

2. How can you find the area of a figure?

3. The area of a figure is measured in what units?

Activity

Use an inch ruler to find the perimeter of the figures below. Then find the area of each.

A

B